The Little Lama of Tibet

LOIS RAIMONDO

SCHOLASTIC INC. NEW YORK

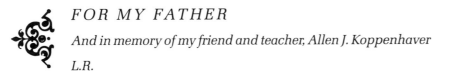

FOR MY FATHER

And in memory of my friend and teacher, Allen J. Koppenhaver

L.R.

I would like to thank His Holiness the Dalai Lama for giving his blessing to this project. I am grateful to Ling Rinpoche, Kunga-la, Tenzing Phuntsok, and the members of Ling Labrang for their hospitality and good company. I would also like to thank Tenzin Geyche-la and Lakpa Dorje in the Office of the Dalai Lama; Thubten Samphel, at the Office of Tibet; T.T. Lingsang, Ruth Sonam, Ngawang Dolma and Tsering Phuntsok, Karma Gelek, Lisa Heath, and K.S. Bagga.

In the United States, thanks to Phoebe Yeh, my editor at Scholastic, who gave good guidance from beginning to end; and Mark Bussell at *The New York Times* for his encouragement. Grateful acknowledgement is made to the University of Missouri School of Journalism and to Dave Metz and his staff at Canon Professional Services. Finally, thanks to my nephew Jon Loukis Raimondo, for having so much compassion in his three-year-old heart. He gives me hope.

I used Canon F-1 camera bodies with the following lenses: 24mm 1:1.4 LD, 28mm 2.8, 35 1.2, 50mm 1:1.2 L, and 135mm 1.28. With the exception of the cover photo and the right-hand picture on p. 22, which were both lit with a Vivitar 283 strobe, all photographs were made with available light.

Library of Congress Cataloging-in-Publication Data
Raimondo, Lois. The little lama of tibet / written and photographed by Lois Raimondo.
p.   cm.
Summary: A biography of Ling Rinpoche, a young monk, who is one of the most highly regarded priests in the Tibetan Buddhist religion.
1. Ling, Rinpoche—Juvenile literature. 2. Lamas—India—Biography—Juvenile literature. 3. Lamas—China—Tibet—Biography—Juvenile literature. [1. Ling, Rinpoche. 2. Lamas. 3. Buddhism—Tibet.] I. Title.
BQ970.I55R35   1994   294.3′923′092—dc20   [B]   93-13627   CIP   AC

ISBN 0-590-46167-2

12 11 10 9 8 7 6 5 4 3 2 1   4 5 6 7 8 9/9
Printed in the U.S.A.   37
First Scholastic printing, February 1994

Calligraphy by Norbu Choephel   Map by Jeanyee Wong   Book design by Kathleen Westray

THE DALAI LAMA

IN *The Little Lama of Tibet*, Lois Raimondo has produced a delightful children's book, based on the story of the reincarnation of my late tutor, Ling Rinpoche.

My own childhood and youth were spent under his watchful care, and even as an adult I continued to look to him for advice. For over forty years, until he passed away in 1983, I regarded him as one of my closest friends. As a teacher he was strict but skillful, for which he earned my respect and gratitude. At the same time, he was full of human warmth. His affection and concern for me were such that I thought of him as a father. It was from his personal example that I learned the importance of developing a sense of purpose and concern for others.

In the Tibetan Buddhist tradition we believe that great teachers are intentionally reborn so that they can continue to be of benefit to others. Accordingly, a search was made for Ling Rinpoche's reincarnation. This bright little boy, found at the Tibetan Children's Village, was recognized as the new incarnation of Ling Rinpoche.

The very basis of someone like Ling Rinpoche's deliberately being reborn in this way, is his profoundly humane concern to help other beings. I hope that this photographic account of Ling Rinpoche's present incarnation will help other children learn something of the importance of that warmhearted kindness that he exemplifies.

Six-year-old Ling Rinpoche (LING RIN-PO-CHAY) lives in the mountains of Dharamsala (DAR-UM-SAL-A), Northern India, with a "family" of twelve teachers, attendants, cooks, housecleaners, and caretakers. Rinpoche is the youngest and most important member of the household.

In some ways, Rinpoche is like many other six-year-olds. But he is also a high lama, one of the most respected priests in the Tibetan Buddhist religion, and that makes him very different.

The Tibetans believe that Ling Rinpoche is much more than one small boy. They believe that in his heart and mind, he holds the wisdom of many great Buddhist teachers who lived so many centuries ago in their native country of Tibet. This is why he is called "Rinpoche." It is the Tibetan word for "precious."

Rinpoche was born in India, but his ancestors are from the neighboring land of Tibet in Western Asia. Tibet is a mountainous country with a culture and religion that is thousands of years old.

Rinpoche's mother died when he was just a baby. His father was a poor farmer. Since he could not afford to take care of Rinpoche, he took the baby to the Tibetan Children's Village in Dharamsala, a home for Tibetan orphans. At the orphanage, the baby was recognized as a lama of great distinction.

Since that time, Rinpoche has always lived apart from ordinary people. Instead, he is surrounded by handpicked attendants as he prepares for the moment when it will be his turn to teach others.

In the Tibetan religious tradition, all living beings—people, plants, and animals—are sacred. This means that every person has the seed of knowledge and spirituality inside his or her own mind. It is up to each individual to develop that potential. From his studies, Rinpoche will learn what he needs to know to help other people develop spiritually.

Every day, Rinpoche's attendant Tenzing Phuntsok (TEN-ZING POON-SOCK) wakes Rinpoche before dawn. After his bath, Rinpoche exercises for thirty minutes. "It is very important," Tenzing Phuntsok explains, "that the body take exercise to keep up with the mind."

Next, Rinpoche dresses in a short-sleeved golden shirt and long maroon robes. Maroon and gold are the only colors that Tibetan monks and nuns wear. The colors represent simplicity and purity. In the summer, Rinpoche wears cool cotton robes. In the winter, the robes are made of wool.

After being served a breakfast of fried eggs, buttered bread, and milk tea, Rinpoche joins his teacher Kunga-la (KOONG-A-LA) in the prayer room. Together, teacher and student pray, asking the gods to bring peace to all people on earth.

Rinpoche learned his first prayer when he was just two years old.
Today, he can recite many prayers by heart.

Each morning, Rinpoche spends two hours reading religious stories out loud with Kunga-la. In one story, a goddess comes to Earth to save the people from terrible dangers. In another story, a farmer befriends a beggar because he knows that people who do good deeds will be rewarded in their next lives. In Rinpoche's favorite stories, animals give advice to people who need help.

In the afternoon, Rinpoche's Tibetan teacher, Lobsang Samten (LOBE-SANG PSALM-TEN) gives him a Tibetan language lesson. Rinpoche has already mastered printing the alphabet. Eventually, he will learn four different ways of writing in script.

Rinpoche's writing tools are simple: a shaved wooden stick and a small bottle of black ink. Rinpoche concentrates hard as he practices, so he usually gets his letters right on the first try. He knows that Lobsang Samten will check each stroke on every page.

Rinpoche's daily lessons are often interrupted by visitors. People come from near and far to visit him because they want to meet the famous young monk. Rinpoche listens patiently to their questions and sometimes gives advice. People are always amazed at how much the little boy knows. On the day a group of worshipers arrive, Rinpoche presents red blessing cords to his guests. The cords symbolize good health, long life, and peace.

Since most visitors cannot speak Tibetan, Rinpoche is also learning
how to speak English and Hindi. When he gets older, he will use these
languages when he travels the world to teach.

"Playing with toys is fun," says Rinpoche, "but studying hard is
much more important. I already know many things, but people need
so many different advices, I must learn more."

In the Tibetan tradition, the most important teachings are always passed directly from teacher to student through the spoken word. Book knowledge is valuable, but Tibetans believe that learning directly from the teacher is most important of all. Both teacher and student have equal responsibilities in the learning process.

In keeping with the teaching tradition, all of Rinpoche's teachers pay careful attention to Rinpoche's language lessons. He learns to read, write, and speak only proper Tibetan and to use good grammar in his English lessons. While Rinpoche is still learning, his contact with outsiders is carefully monitored so that he cannot pick up any bad habits.

One of Rinpoche's favorite visitors is Kyabje Trijang (KEY-OPP-J TREE-JONG), a twelve-year-old boy who also is a high lama. Trijang lives in a monastery in Mundgod (MUND-GOOD), deep in Southern India. Mundgod is a five-day journey by car and train to Dharamsala, where Rinpoche lives. Since both lamas are so busy with their studies and responsibilities, they are only able to see each other once a year.

When the boys first meet, they gently touch heads, the most intimate form of Tibetan greeting. After he blesses all the attendants, Rinpoche calls for tea and snacks. Finally it's time to play!

When the weather turns cooler,
Rinpoche travels to Bodh Gaya
(BODE GUY-A), where it is warmer.

Bodh Gaya is a sacred Buddhist city with many temples and prayer halls. Rinpoche has his own monastery in Bodh Gaya. Twenty-five monks take care of it when he is living in Dharamsala.

In the evening, just before dinner, Rinpoche walks to the main temple with his attendants. He passes out small coins and sweets to the needy people he meets along the way.

The worshipers have already gathered at the temple. They read prayer books, visit shrines, and light incense at the altars. But when Rinpoche arrives, everyone rushes to greet him. They hold their hands together, their heads bowed down with respect. Many people have used their life savings to make the long journey to the holy city of Bodh Gaya. A chance to see Rinpoche in person is a tremendous honor, and many shed tears of joy.

Rinpoche walks through the temple grounds. He blesses a small boy by gently placing his hands on the top of his head. As Rinpoche turns the prayer wheels, each revolution carries his prayers to heaven. Then Rinpoche bows his head to the ancient prayer books on the altar to show respect for the knowledge that they contain. One day he will study from these same texts.

On special holy days, Rinpoche sits on a golden throne and leads
hundreds of people in prayer. Monks, nuns, and ordinary people
gather together to pray as one voice. The Tibetans believe that by
praying in unison, they will strengthen the request. A ceremony can
last for as long as five hours. But Rinpoche says that he does not get
tired because he is the leader and all the people are watching him.

Rinpoche gets some help from Tenzing Phuntsok, who sits on the ground at the side of the throne. Tenzing Phuntsok reminds Rinpoche if he forgets to ring the religious bell or bang the drum at just the right moment.

The day after a ceremony, Rinpoche is allowed some extra playtime.

Since Rinpoche does not really have any friends his own age, his playmates are his teachers, attendants, and cooks.

Rinpoche is a young boy with lots of energy and his caretakers are elderly. But when Rinpoche asks them to play, even if they are tired, they will agree. They want him to be happy.

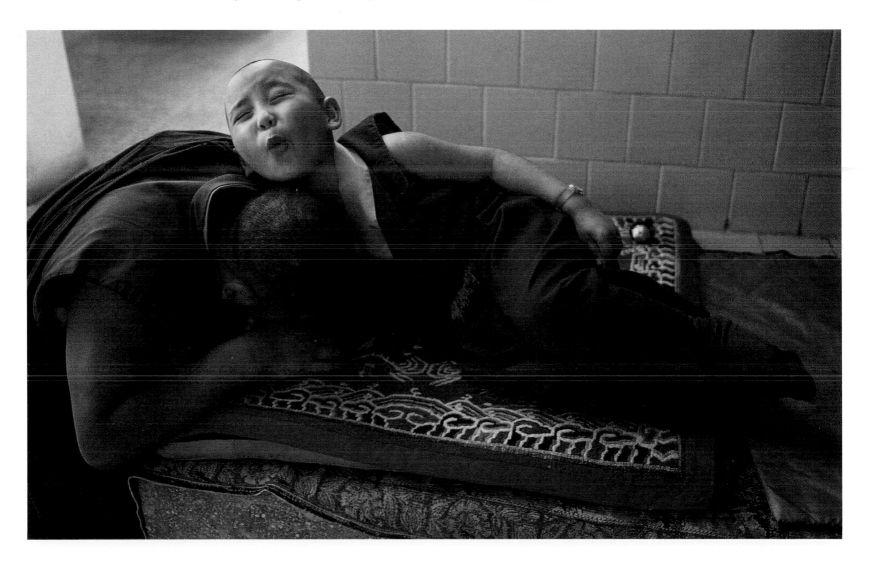

Throughout the year, Rinpoche works hard at his studies while his attendants are busy caring for him. Once a year everyone goes on vacation in New Delhi. For one week, Rinpoche eats strawberry ice cream, watches cartoons on television, *and* he doesn't have to study.

When Rinpoche turns ten, he will go to live at Drepung Loseling Monastery (DRAY-POONG LOW-SE-LING) in Mundgod, Southern India. He will study with the most knowledgeable teachers and learn all he can about Buddhism and the world.

One day Rinpoche will teach others. People will come from
all over the world to hear his teachings. Not all of them will be
Buddhist. Each person will take away something different
from the lesson, but everyone will learn from Rinpoche.

Ling Rinpoche is a precious symbol to the Tibetan people. Since many Tibetans now live outside Tibet, in foreign countries, they worry that the practice of Tibetan ways will be lost and that Tibet will be forgotten.

But when they see Ling Rinpoche leading prayer ceremonies, studying Tibetan scriptures, and giving blessings with such great kindness, they gain new hope. They know that Tibet is still very much alive.

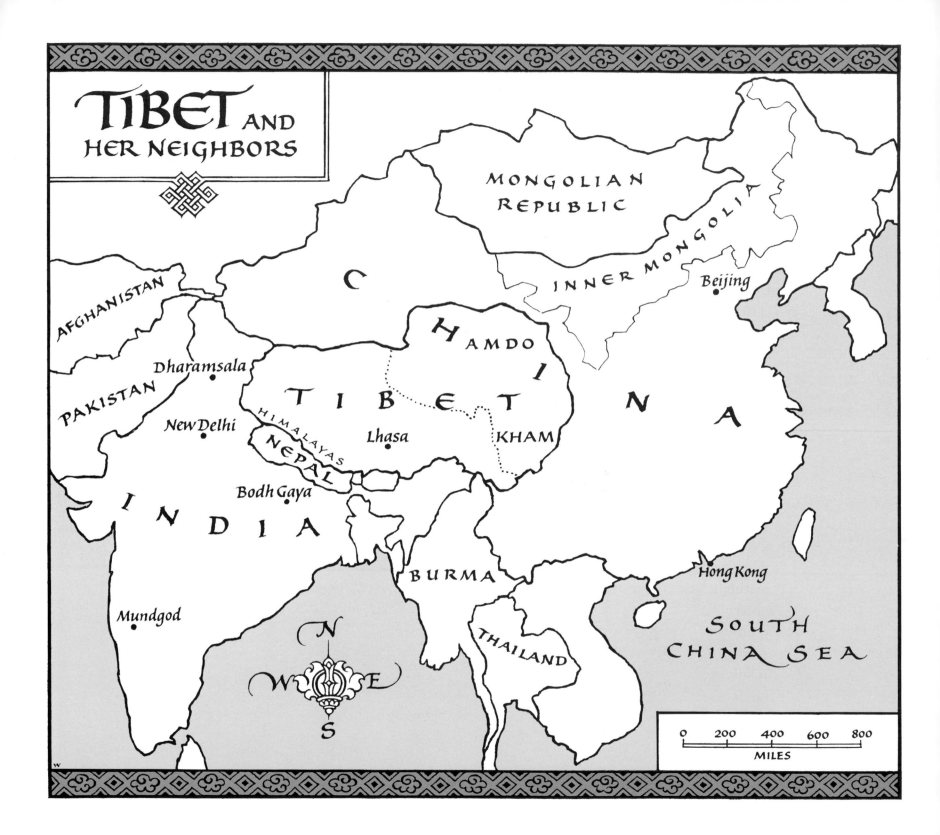

TIBET AND HER NEIGHBORS

MONGOLIAN REPUBLIC

INNER MONGOLIA

Beijing

AFGHANISTAN

PAKISTAN

Dharamsala

C H I N A

AMDO

New Delhi

TIBET

HIMALAYAS

NEPAL

Lhasa

KHAM

Bodh Gaya

INDIA

BURMA

Mundgod

THAILAND

Hong Kong

SOUTH CHINA SEA

N
W E
S

0   200   400   600   800
MILES

MORE ABOUT TIBET

TIBET is a high, mountainous country that contains some of the world's most spectacular natural beauty. With an average altitude of 4,880 meters (16,000 feet) above sea level, Tibet's snow-covered Himalayan peaks rise up against deep blue skies. Almost as large as Western Europe in area, its neighbors are India, China, and Nepal.

For thousands of years, Tibet was isolated from the rest of the world. Fearing the influence of outsiders, Tibet's succession of leaders, the Dalai Lamas, would not allow foreigners to enter their land.

In 1950, the Chinese government began sending military troops into Tibet. Five years later, China reshaped the borders of Tibet, incorporating Kham and Amdo (eastern and north-eastern Tibet) into their neighboring Chinese provinces. On March 10, 1959, the Chinese army invaded the capital city of Lhasa and officially occupied the country of Tibet. The occupiers quickly set to their stated task of "liberating the locals from their feudal past." Their real intention was to eliminate the practice of Buddhism, which would lead to the disappearance of Tibetan culture.

Since that time, more than 1.2 million Tibetans, more than one fifth of the entire population, have died. Over six thousand monasteries have been destroyed. Today, only twelve monasteries remain intact. More than one hundred thousand Tibetans, including Ling Rinpoche and the Dalai Lama, are now living as refugees in the neighboring lands of India and Nepal.

When the Dalai Lama escaped to India, thirty-four years ago, he immediately set to work rebuilding Tibetan culture in exile. Monasteries, schools, orphanages, craft cooperatives, and farming communities have been established for Tibetan refugees in India and Nepal.

In spite of intense repression and persecution, the Buddhist religion continues to be the focal point of Tibetan life. And, it is the hope of the Tibetans that one day soon, they will be able to return to their homeland. In the meantime, it is the responsibility of cultural caretakers like young Ling Rinpoche to ensure that the Tibetan way of life can continue in exile.

When asked if there was anything Ling Rinpoche wanted to tell American children, he replied:

"I have so, SO many advices to give the American children! I have many things that I would like to tell you.
Number one: Everyone should study very hard.
Number two: You should respect your teachers and take action according to the teachers' advices.

Number three: Children should always obey their mother and father and listen to what they say. Children who have parents must be very kind to those who don't [have parents]. They must take special care of orphaned children because they need love, too.

We should offer things [to the needy], and always try to help those who are less fortunate than we are. We should always act wisely to come back as better lives.

And now, I have some advice for the big people, not for the children. To the mother and father I say, when you have your child you must be very, very kind to the child. And when the child grows up he will repay the parents and take so much very good care of them their whole life. This way they are very kind to each other. And thus, we create great kindness in the world."

The Tibetan Alphabet *(below)*

Tibetan Vowels and Consonants *(right)*